Also by Bill Berger

What to do with a Dead Lawyer

What to do with a

Dead
Boomer

Shopping Gift Catalog: Winter, 2027

BY BILL BERGER

ILLUSTRATIONS ~ JAKE FULLER

COVER ART ~ RICARDO MARTINEZ

GRAPHIC DESIGN ~ BRANDON YOWELL

A BERGER BOOKS PUBLICATION

Berger Books
Contact: aBergerBook@gmail.com

ISBN-13: 978-0692508794

What to do
with a
Dead
Boomer

Shopping Gift Catalog: Winter, 2027

INTER-GALACTIC SALVAGE

Memo

INTER-GALACTIC SALVAGE

DEDICATED TO EXPLOITING THE UNIVERSE

I.G.

$

SALVAGE

OUR MOTTO: FINDERS, KEEPERS

FROM THE DESK OF: 9R5 O' Zyrx,
Project Manager, EARTH PROJECT

TO: 2H7 Broznor, Director of Operations,
INTER-GALACTIC SALVAGE

DATE: 3rd Minor of Tremor,
Veron

SUBJECT: DEAD BOOMERS

PRAISE COMMERCE!

Boss, here's the latest on Artifact 78-39 discovered in the Earth Dig Site. Turns out it's a shopping gift catalog called **What to do with a Dead Boomer** published long ago in the Classo era (year 2027 using Earth dating). The guys in Anthropology say it shows Humans once practiced a bizarre form of **Commerce**. We're calling it the Dead Boomer Cult.

THE HISTORY OF BABY BOOMERS

To understand the Dead Boomer Cult, let me rehash what we know about **Baby Boomers**.

Our scholars have long known of a subspecies of the Human Race known as Baby Boomers that dominated the planet Earth for a while until they suddenly died off.

We know their name is derived from a combination of their lifelong immaturity and their loud, pushy, self-centered, obnoxious manners. Think of a demanding, colicky child barking like the horn on a **Maximus GT7000 Continent Excavator**.

Baby Boomers had a peculiar life cycle filled with extreme changes and contradictions. It seems they couldn't make up their minds what they wanted to be.

Boomers were pampered early on by their parents, then entered a stage of life when they rebelled against everything their parents stood for.

What particularly shocked their elders was the attitude Boomers had for the peculiar Human joining ritual called **sex**. For some reason we still haven't discovered, their parents didn't want to talk about sex; Boomers wouldn't shut up about it.

But for us, the most important thing about this life cycle phase of Baby Boomers was their rejection of the **Supreme Urge**.

The Supreme Urge—the urge to acquire and hoard everything you can get your tentacles around--is, of course, found in all intelligent life forms throughout the Galaxies. It's why we're intelligent. Any sentient being who rejects the Supreme Urge is sick and a threat to Commerce.

Boomers at this stage of their lives rebelled and protested against anything having to do with Commerce.

The authorities on Earth were weak. Can you imagine Boomers trying to get away with this nonsense on, say, **Attaxa 5** or **Uuuuuuu**?

Anywhere else but Earth the moment a bunch of them started chanting their anti-hoarding crap they'd have been crushed like a **buzzgut**.

It was during this life cycle phase that Earth, a mere speck of a crumb of a planet, became a security concern for us.

They had developed nuclear weapons, but who cared? Let them blow themselves up! Then they discovered space travel.

The clincher was the emergence of Baby Boomers in their anti-hoarding stage (called **Hippies** and then an even more virulent form, **Yippies**). If they took control of Earth, who could predict the havoc to Commerce such a race might cause?

After our spies, disguised as cows (a form of Earth animal which unfortunately for some of our agents we didn't know was used for consumption), had reported all this, the Galactic Fleet was placed on High Alert.

The only thing that saved Earth from immediate destruction was the sudden metamorphosis of Baby Boomers into their next life cycle phase.

Why Boomers evolved into this next phase is unknown. We know it coincided with their entering the childbearing stage of life when they acquired something called a **mortgage**. Whatever the reason, what saved their miserable planet from annihilation was that Baby Boomers, miraculously for everyone on Earth, now **embraced** the Supreme Urge, and in a big way.

From then on, Baby Boomers (now called **Yuppies** and then **real estate developers**) took off on an unquenchable hoarding binge that lasted the rest of their lives.

THE GREAT BOOMER DIE-OFF

Boomers were the first generation on Earth to grow up watching **television**, a primitive device which provided rudimentary visual and audio entertainment.

Their parents discovered young Boomers were transfixed by television images, giving rise to the widespread practice of leaving them in front of televisions for long periods.

Televisions originally broadcasted images in black and white. During Boomers' formative years, a manufacturer introduced the first color televisions. In no time there were millions of color sets on Earth with a young Boomer or two in front of every one.

Unfortunately, as we now know from spectrum analyses of the Boomer fossil record, these early color televisions emitted lethal rays.

Recent archaeological studies have shown the most dangerous sets were those in use during the years two shows, "**The Wonderful World of Disney**" and "**Bonanza**," were popular with young Baby Boomers. Color saturated images from those shows gave off unusually high concentrations of deadly rays.

Tragically, thinking they were providing their children innocent, mindless entertainment, Boomers' parents were actually sealing their doom.

The long-term, slow acting effect of this exposure manifested itself in Boomers late in their lives. This led to a sudden mass Boomer Die-Off in Earth-year 2025 when they dropped like **ennns**.

WHAT TO DO WITH THEM?

With the **Great Boomer Die-Off**, Earth was inundated with dead Baby Boomers and had to face the dilemma of getting rid of them.

One thing Boomers had become good at was **product branding**. They were whizzes at it, on a par with the **Merchants of Veenor**. The appeal of branding is something everyone in Commerce can relate to.

We're all familiar with the tendency of consumers throughout the Universe to buy anything that has a clever brand name. Remember when every kid in the **Hydox System** just had to have a **Yap Yap Yap-Nip Doll**?

Boomers passed on the knack for branding to their children who passed it on to theirs. An entrepreneur quickly cornered the market on dead Baby Boomers and sold them under the catchy brand name **Dead Boomer Products**. Soon, everyone had to have one.

THE DEAD BOOMER CULT

Artifact 78-39 confirms that Dead Boomer Products became wildly popular. There must have been a craze for them. We call it the "Dead Boomer Cult."

When you think of it, the Dead Boomer Cult represents an extremely imaginative, I'd even say unique, manifestation of the Supreme Urge. It's the only instance we know of anywhere in the Galaxies where a race has marketed the dead bodies of its elders as consumer products. You've got to give it to the inventive genius who came up with that idea.

Boss, check out the restored **Artifact 78-39** accompanying this memo.

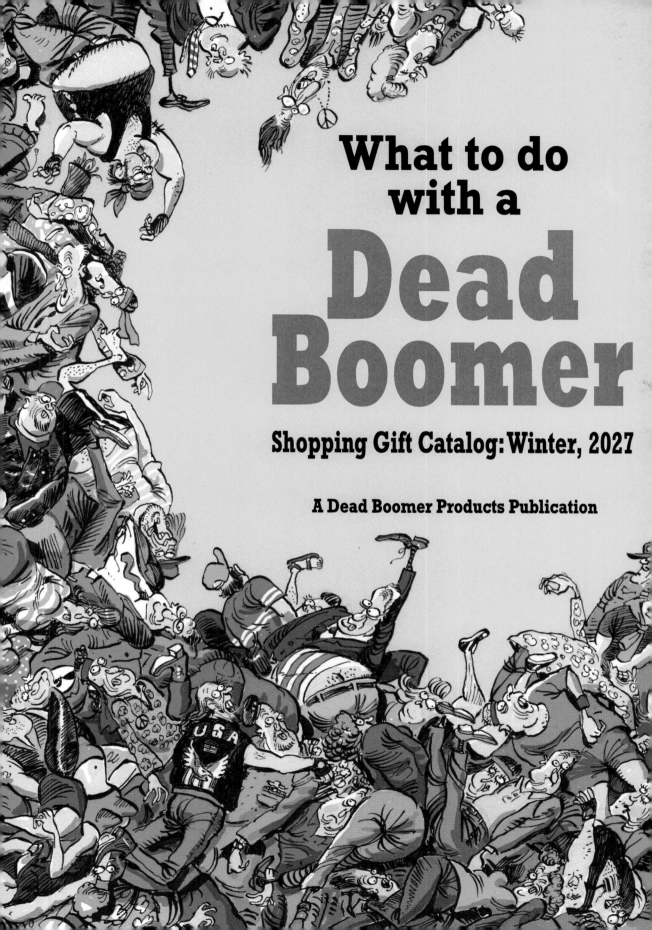

What to do with a

Dead Boomer

Shopping Gift Catalog: Winter, 2027

A Dead Boomer Products Publication

"Season's Greetings" to Our Valued Customers!
The Story Behind Dead Boomer Products

When my wife, Twirl, and I founded Dead Boomer Products a year ago, we had one simple goal in mind: to find a safe, natural and tasteful use for all those dead Baby Boomers piling up everywhere, one that didn't just solve the greatest health crisis in world history but also kept alive the memory of their unique Boomer lifestyle and tradition.

Glin and Twirl Gulinney, Founders, Dead Boomer Products

Call them irresponsible. Call them conceited. Call them smug, pretentious, ostentatious, pompous, superficial, sanctimonious, egotistical, greedy, vain, shallow and narcissistic.

But how can you not love 'em? Baby Boomers had that forever young *je ne sais quoi*, that attitude and look that said with a vengeance, I'm better off than you.

Twirl was so moved by the sight of all those Dead Boomers she was inspired to pen her classic song, *Where Have All the Boomers Gone?*, "gone" meaning, of course, in the spiritual sense. After all, even a blind man could tell where they were physically, assuming he could smell.

And when she sang it to win American Topless Idol, well, she certainly struck a nerve in the public, as we all know. We've had Dead Boomer Products flying off our shelves ever since.

Twirl and I get a lot of inquiries asking how we do it. How do we take the body of, say, a dead old fart and turn him into the Adonis he once was? Or the shriveled husk of a bag lady and give her back those lap dancer looks that put bacon on the table in her youth? The theoretical basis for what we do is really quite simple.

Our genes never grow old. Instead, they go through age cycles, like a clock winding down. As long as the old fart really was handsome and the bag lady really was hot poon way back when, using our patented Reverse Genetic Engineering, we can reset their genes, like rewinding a clock back to the appropriate time in their lives. We then carefully hang our Dead Boomers in a temperature controlled, refrigerated environment and leave them until they achieve the right age.

Treated with special restorative enzymes and fluids to render them malleable, soon they can be manipulated (enlarged, shrunken, stretched) like warm wax using our shaping technology to whatever form we need for their intended purpose.

We're committed to quality here at Dead Boomer Products. All our Dead Boomers are made with your satisfaction in mind.

And rest assured: no Boomer has suffered in the manufacturing process.

We are pleased to offer this collection of Dead Boomer Products for Winter, 2027. You'll find their classic Boomer functionality and looks just the thing for the Holidays.

Why wait? This Holiday Season bring happiness to family and friends with a Dead Boomer Product.

Remember, look for the "**DBP**" branded on the ass. If it's not there, it may be dead, but it's not a genuine Dead Boomer Product and in three months you may have a pile of putrefied flesh on your hands.

And in the best Baby Boomer tradition, be sure you get a Dead Boomer gift or two for the most extra special person in your life: **You**.

Thanks for your patronage!

GLIN GULINNEY

Glin Gulinney, Founder
Dead Boomer Products

Inside find Dead Boomers for:

- Home
- Work
- Play
- On the Go
- And MORE!

AND NOW PRESENTING . . .

FROM OUR DEAD BOOMER HIPPIE COLLECTION

Before they became money-grubbing conformists, Baby Boomers were Hippies. Furry, loveable and simple-minded, Hippies frolicked in the sun, and, at times, the mud. They smoked dope, listened to music, and protested against... everything.

Relive those carefree Hippie days with gifts from our Dead Boomer Hippie Collection.

SMOKE A CLASSIC DEAD BOOMER JOINT FROM OUR SPECIAL STASH

TIRED OF SPACE TRAVEL?

HAD ENOUGH OF THE SHUTTLE?

THEN TAKE A TRIP

INSIDE YOUR MIND

WITH A DEAD BOOMER JOINT.

By using only Dead Boomers certified to have lived the years 1967-69 in the Haight-Ashbury neighborhood of San Francisco, we can assure you our freeze-dried and ground Dead Boomer mixture has a high potency blend of THC, peyote, mescaline and LSD.

DON'T BOGART THAT BOOMER!

HAVE A DEAD BOOMER HIPPIE RAP SESSION

Hippie Boomers loved to sit around and "rap," that is, talk aimlessly about nothing while high on dope. You can recreate those wonderful moments in your own home with our Dead Boomer Hippie Rap Session. Set includes four fully programmable Dead Boomer Hippies. You can adjust their settings from "got a buzz on" all the way to "fuck'n A, my face is melting!" Enjoy hours of saying "bummer," "peace, man," "I'm tripping," and "right on," while laughing hysterically.

PLAY WITH OUR DEAD BOOMER HIPPIE COMMUNE

Wouldn't it be great if you never grew up? Now you can shirk your responsibilities and waste hours and hours by playing with our Dead Boomer Hippie Commune. We've miniaturized a whole colony of Hippie Boomers dressed in authentic Hippie garb. Fun for the whole family.

TAKE A DEAD BOOMER HIPPIE ROAD TRIP

For Boomers, the Road Trip was the ultimate rite of passage. Historians trace the origin of the Road Trip back thousands of years to Homer's Ulysses. Then there was Huckleberry Finn. But Hippie Boomers perfected the Road Trip, as they set out to "discover America," attend an anti-war "Mobe" rally or a five day rock concert. Experience the lure of the road with the Dead Boomer Hippie Road Trip.

Through our Forming Technology, we use Dead Boomers to create replicas of broken down VW vans and refurbished school buses covered with psychedelic paintings. Then we pump them full of marijuana smoke so that every time you open them they have that like-new Dead Boomer smell.

FROM OUR DEAD BOOMER
ROCK MUSIC COLLECTION

Baby Boomers loved their music. It defined them. They called it "Rock 'n Roll," "Rock," "Psychedelic Rock," "Acid Rock," "British Rock," "Electric Rock," "Garage Rock," "Blues Rock," "Hard Rock," and when it became totally old fashioned, "Classic Rock." Boomers thought it was the best music ever. And they not only listened to their music all the time, they listened to the same songs all the time. Can you say, "Stairway to Heaven"?

DEAD BOOMER HEADPHONES

Advances in medical science have enabled us to locate and tap into the Classic Rock music stored in Dead Boomers' memory banks. When you wear our Dead Boomer Headphones, it's like having your own Classic Rock radio station with you all the time!

DEAD BOOMER ROCK STARS

Boomer Rock Stars were the heroes of the generation for which music was king. At concerts attended by hundreds of thousands of fans, Boomer Rockers entertained stoned audiences with songs about social oppression, society's underdogs, and class struggle—all the while raking in untold millions from ticket and album sales, T-shirts, posters and memorabilia.

DEAD BOOMER ROCK STAR GROUPIES

With names like Vivid, Zap and Blue, Boomer groupies--female hangers-on who freely gave their sexual favors to Boomer Rockers--were a fixture around Rock performances. Don't just fantasize about groupies, live the dream with our Dead Boomer Rock Star Groupie Set. Experience the thrill of being plaster casted! Full action set of four.

PRACTICE SKEET SHOOTING WITH OUR DEAD BOOMER DIVAS

With typical Boomer presumptuousness, female Boomer Rock and Pop singers took on the overblown title of "Divas." Their claims to greatness often rested on their fans' addled memories of their early hits. Later, when their talents faded and they needed other means to gain public attention, these Boomer Divas couldn't resist expounding naïve, insipid views on politics, personal relationships and the environment, despite their ignorance of the issues and their own wasteful and destructive lifestyles.

We've turned these exasperating warblers into kiln-hardened skeets for that restful day at the shooting range.

FROM OUR DEAD BOOMER NEW AGE COLLECTION

THE NEW AGE FAIR

Baby Boomers rejected traditional, organized religion. Yet for all their bombast, they still had a need for spiritual guidance. Some crafty Boomers took advantage of this spiritual void to create a money-making venture called New Age Religion, featuring the belief in "The Age of Aquarius" (named after a song title, thus demonstrating just how superficial and fundamentally commercial this movement was). Soon, the Boomer landscape was filled with New Age shops, festivals and fairs.

HAVE YOUR OWN SIGNS OF EXTRATERRESTRIAL LIFE!

New Age Religion relied of the flimsiest of logic and reasoning. New Age devotees weren't just far out in their thinking; they were remote. Take the most innocent form of human phenomena, crop circles, for example. These couldn't have been created by painstaking human endeavor; no, New Age logic dictated that they had to have been made by creatures from another planet.

You can have your own Signs of Extraterrestrial Life with our Dead Boomer Easter Island Statues.

FROM OUR DEAD BOOMER SELF-AWARENESS COLLECTION

"FIND YOURSELF" WITH A DEAD BOOMER SHRINK

Sigmund Freud said, "Sometimes a cigar is just a cigar." Tell that to a Baby Boomer! Their generation sought "true meaning" and was obsessed with self-analysis, introspection, and figuring out who they "really" were and what they "really" wanted to do with their lives. For Boomers, the greatest sin was to be "alienated" from your "true self" so that you never achieved "actualization." Instead, their goal was to "find" themselves. Consult with one of our Dead Boomer Shrinks and be on your own way to becoming "authentic." So realistic you'll think he's really listening to you!

FROM OUR DEAD BOOMER MEN'S FASHION COLLECTION

THE DEAD BOOMER SWEATER LOOK

Boomers set the bar for fashion. And the distinctive male Boomer look was the sweater worn casually over the shoulders with the sleeves tied loosely in front. Do it one better: Wear a Dead Boomer with a sweater over his shoulders hanging over your shoulders with his arms tied loosely in front of you! A real head turner!

THE DEAD BOOMER PROFESSIONAL SAMPLER

The ultimate Holiday Gift for the Dead Boomer connoisseur: our sampler collection of Dead Boomer Professionals. Includes a doctor, lawyer, accountant, chiropractor, psychologist, engineer and sexologist.

FROM OUR DEAD BOOMER PET COLLECTION

Boomers pampered their pets as much as their children. Pets were an indispensable addition to the Boomer family and in many cases a substitute for children. We feature some items that are sure to please your pet.

DEAD BOOMER SCRATCHING POST

What cat wouldn't love to run its claws against our Dead Boomer Scratching Post? Help Kitty sharpen her nails while keeping her away from your furniture!

DEAD BOOMER LITTER BOX

Want to really get on your cat's good side? Your cat can put in our custom designed litter box what most Boomers were full of!

FROM OUR DEAD BOOMER
FITNESS COLLECTION

Boomers were fitness fanatics. They made sweat a fashion statement. Stay in shape the Dead Boomer way.

DEAD BOOMER AEROBICS CLASS

Lead a workout with the generation that invented the workout! You be the aerobics instructor to a class of buffed and beautified Dead Boomers. Our Dead Boomer Aerobics Class includes a set of five fully mobile Dead Boomers clad in the most stylish leotards, leggings and exercise togs.

DEAD BOOMER BICYCLE CLUB

For all their talk about "individuality," Boomers loved a crowd. And they loved to be noticed in a crowd. Combine Boomers' herd mentality with vigorous exercise and an attention attracting fashion statement with the Dead Boomer Bicycle Club.

FROM OUR DEAD BOOMER OUTDOOR ADVENTURE COLLECTION

When that playwright Shakespeare said, "The world is my oyster," he must have had Baby Boomers in mind. No generation has laid claim to all the world has to offer like Boomers. They notched up outdoor adventures like a hooker does tricks.

SCALE MT. EVEREST WITH A DEAD BOOMER OXYGEN TANK

Yuppie Boomers considered scaling Mt. Everest one of the things you just had to do before you died. Now let a Dead Boomer help you climb to the top of the

world! We arrange it all: your transportation to Nepal, your equipment and your Sherpa guides. And you'll be aided on your trek to the summit by our Dead Boomer Oxygen Tanks. Extra light weight, compact construction with maximum capacity. Don't "hold your breath" waiting to purchase these as quantities are limited.

HANG TEN ON A DEAD BOOMER SURFBOARD

Early surfers were homeless and penniless. Boomers transformed the sport from a local native pastime into a worldwide fad. With their uncanny ability to see a profit in every human endeavor, Boomers created a whole industry, from professional surfers to clothing manufacturers to travel agents to songwriters and countless others feeding off the surfing craze.

Satisfy your Jones for a tasty pipeline run through the barrel and push aside those wave hogs with a Dead Boomer Surfboard.

DEAD BOOMER POLO STICKS

A day at the Polo field was the ultimate status symbol for sports-minded Boomer spectators. And owning a string of polo horses and sponsoring your own team said that you had arrived. Our Polo Sticks are made from eviscerated, titanium reinforced Dead Boomers to ensure a lightweight but powerful swing.

FROM OUR DEAD BOOMER
FAMILY COLLECTION

Vanity pervaded Boomer family life. In perverse contrast to the lack of attention shown them by their parents, Boomers turned their children into status symbols.

DEAD BOOMER SOCCER MOMS

From burning bras to wearing WonderBras, how did the generation of females who founded the Feminist Movement become the Soccer Mom generation? Whatever. Our Dead Boomer Soccer Moms are programmed to be "buds" to your kids, pick them up from school, chauffeur them to after- school activities and talk endlessly to other moms about where your kids will attend college.

DEAD BOOMER SCHOOL BAGS

Doting Boomer parents made sure their young ones went to school in the height of fashion. With our Dead Boomer School Bags, your child will never be "bored of education"!

THE DEAD BOOMER
DYSFUNCTIONAL HOME REALITY SHOW

Who doesn't enjoy watching those senseless Reality Shows? Did you know they were invented by Boomers? You can have your own Dysfunctional Dead Boomer Family perform endlessly for you in your home. We've fashioned our Dead Boomers into dead ringers of classic Boomer reality show families. Invite your friends over to watch the tireless antics of the Kardashians, the Osbourns, and the Real Housewives. Buy them one at a time or an entire family.

FROM OUR DEAD BOOMER LIFESTYLES COLLECTION

DEAD BOOMER JUMPERS

Stressed out? Ever feel like jumping off a building, things are so bad? Let a Dead Boomer do it for you. Our Dead Boomer Jumpers are carefully selected from internet day traders. Just find a tall building and throw your Dead Boomer Jumper off the top. You'll feel a whole lot better!

DEAD BOOMER SEX TOYS

How's your love life lately? Don't ask? Well, we can make it a whole lot better with our handy Dead Boomer Sex Toys. Carry one wherever you go. You'll have people asking, are you happy to see me or is that a Dead Boomer in your pocket?

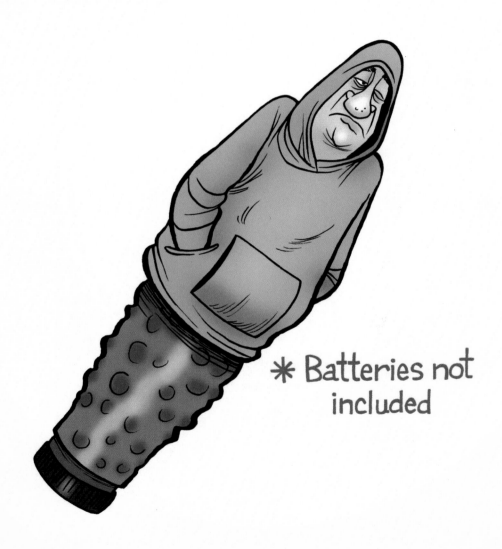

* Batteries not included

CREATE THAT SPECIAL MOOD WITH DEAD BOOMER CANDLES

Boomers loved candles. From grungy dorm rooms and flea ridden apartments to 15,000 square foot McMansions, Boomers had candles everywhere. Get in that special Boomer mood with our Dead Boomer Candles. Scented or unscented.

DEAD BOOMER VIRTUAL REALITY HEADSETS

For that ultimate Virtual Reality experience, don't just wear a headset. Wear a Dead Boomer's head!

We've sourced our headsets from subjects who participated in Dr. Timothy Leary's Harvard Psilocybin Project and early experiments with LSD.

Computer graphics don't come close. You'll experience the real thing when you immerse yourself in the sights, sounds and sensations stored in the lobes of brains steeped in psychedelia with our Dead Boomer Virtual Reality Headsets.

Get a Head for your Head, for that HEAD in you!

FROM OUR DEAD BOOMER "LOOK AT ME" COLLECTION

Boomers turned their parents' goal of "keeping up with the Joneses" into a quest to outdo them.

DEAD BOOMER ON BOARD SIGNS

Draw attention to yourself and at the same time pay tribute to the generation that made narcissism an art form with the "Dead Boomer on Board" sign

DEAD BOOMER SHIT

It's no exaggeration to say that Boomers thought their shit didn't stink. You be the judge.

Tastefully wrapped.

ORDER NOW!

THESE DEAD BOOMERS WON'T LAST LONG.

INTER-GALACTIC SALVAGE
Memo

INTER-GALACTIC SALVAGE

DATE: 3rd Minor of Tremor,
Veron

SUBJECT: DEAD BOOMERS (continued)

P.S., Boss,

It would have been interesting to see how long Dead Boomer Products could have continued as a commercial success. Unfortunately, soon after the publication of Artifact 78-39 in 2027, Earth entered its Second Ice Age, which resulted in the extinction of the human race.

PRAISE COMMERCE!

Made in the USA
Middletown, DE
13 May 2020